Easy Piano

BARLOW & BEAR

the unofficial
BRIDGERTON
MUSICAL

HAL•LEONARD®

Visit Hal Leonard Online at **www.halleonard.com**

"Bridgerton®" is a registered trademark of Netflix Studios, LLC.

ISBN 978-1-70515-567-7

Contact us:
Hal Leonard
7777 West Bluemound Road
Milwaukee, WI 53213
Email: info@halleonard.com

In Europe, contact:
Hal Leonard Europe Limited
42 Wigmore Street
Marylebone, London, W1U 2RN
Email: info@halleonardeurope.com

In Australia, contact:
Hal Leonard Australia Pty. Ltd.
4 Lentara Court
Cheltenham, Victoria, 3192 Australia
Email: info@halleonard.com.au

STORY OF BRIDGERTON THE MUSICAL

After the Netflix smash hit regency romance series graced our screens, Abigail Barlow and Emily Bear set out to answer the simple question: What if Bridgerton was a musical? They answered by writing and composing 15 original songs in six weeks, live on social media. Featuring lead vocals by Barlow, the album was produced and orchestrated by Bear, who sings additional vocals.

With #BridgertonMusical reaching more than 240 million views, and with 48 million likes between them, Barlow and Bear have released The Unofficial Bridgerton Musical, a concept album based on Bridgerton's first season. The response has been spectacular, with the album hitting #1 on iTunes U.S. Pop Albums within two hours of its release, Top 5 worldwide, and has been nominated for a Grammy Award®.

Bear (19) and Barlow (22) are two young women who have independently carved out their own space in the musical theater world. Barlow was a founding creator on TikTok and has a flourishing singer-songwriter career with the chart success of her independently-released pop hit "Heartbreak Hotel." Meanwhile, Bear has had a rich career as an award-winning composer and piano prodigy who first appeared on The Ellen DeGeneres Show at age six, and has performed around the world including Carnegie Hall and Lincoln Center. Although individually accomplished, together the pair are breathing new life into musical theater with The Unofficial Bridgerton Musical's merging of Broadway influences, contemporary scoring and a pop through-line.

Barlow and Bear's creative process ushers in a new-founded feat: live streaming on TikTok and Instagram to transparently involve their audience in every step of making this album. Demystifying the creative process with real-time live-streams documenting their composing, orchestrating and recording sessions, Barlow and Bear have broken the glass ceiling on how musicals become mainstream.

CONTENTS

'TIS THE SEASON

Words and Music by EMILY BEAR
and ABIGAIL BARLOW

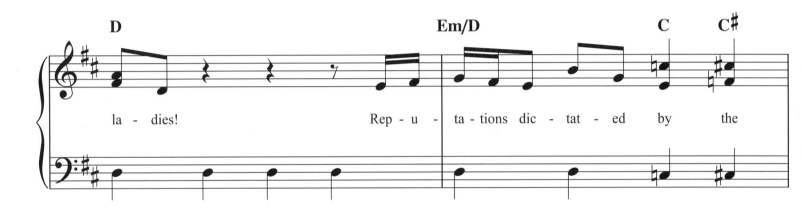

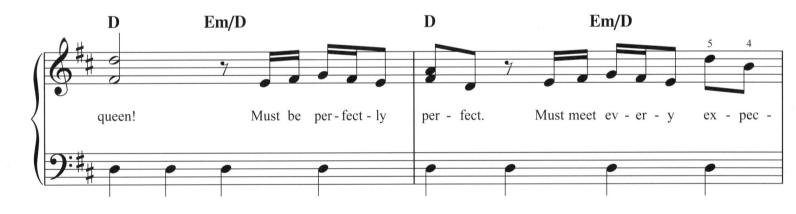

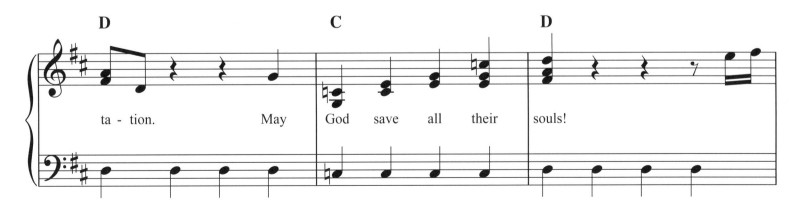

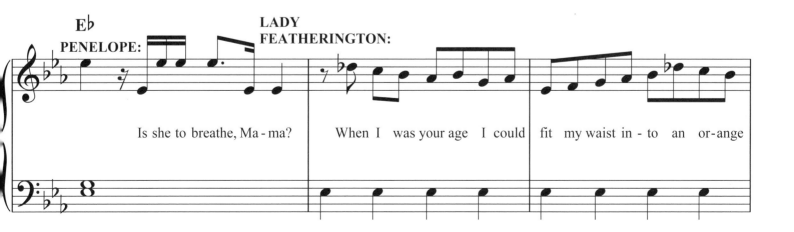

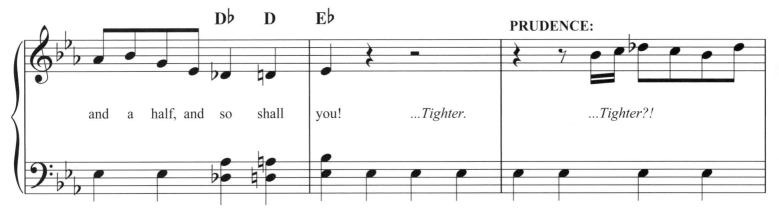

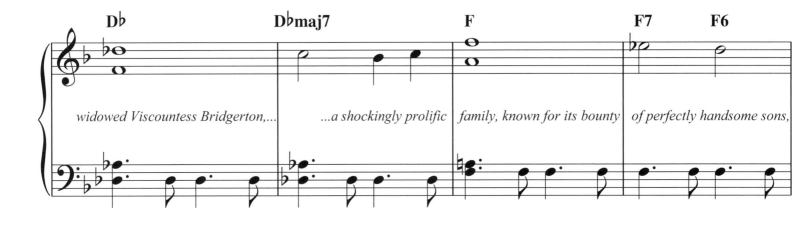

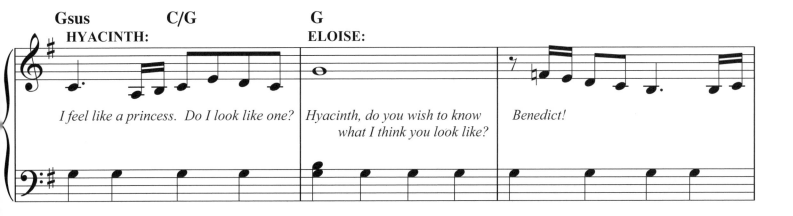

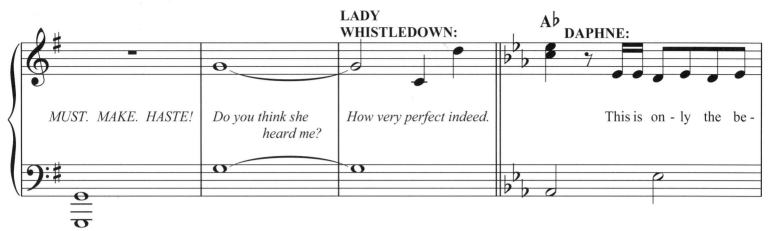

MUST. MAKE. HASTE! | Do you think she heard me? | How very perfect indeed. | This is on-ly the be-

LADY WHISTLEDOWN:

DAPHNE:

gin - ning | of the life that I'll be liv - ing. I'm dream-ing of a

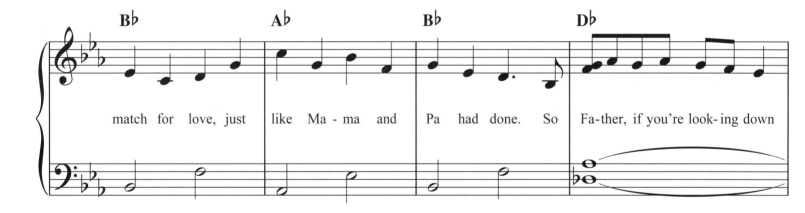

match for love, just | like Ma - ma and | Pa had done. So | Fa-ther, if you're look-ing down

from a-bove, | I'm mar-ry-ing for love. | 'Tis the

THE SOCIETY:

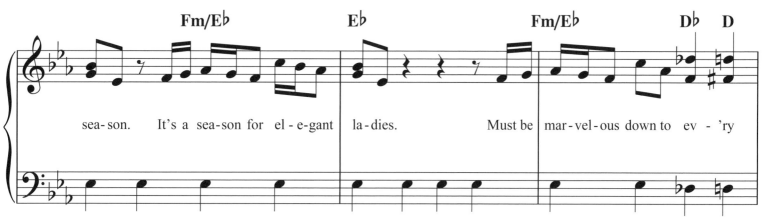

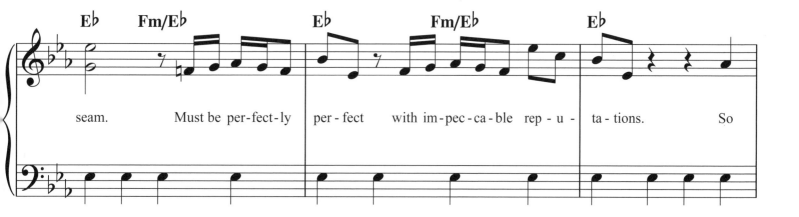

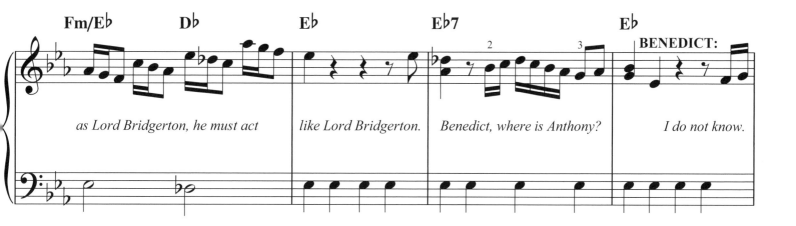

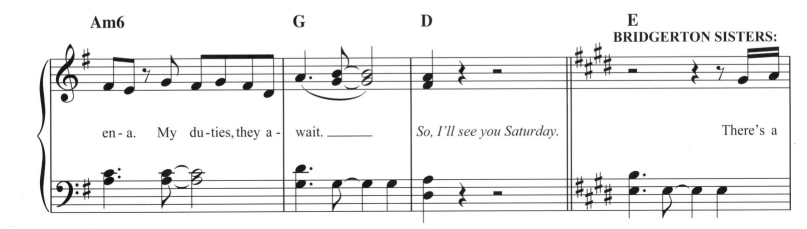

reason, there's a rea-son for all of this cra-zy. The on-ly word that mat-ters is the

queens's.

LADY WHISTLEDOWN:

Today is a most important *day;* *and for some,* *a terrifying one.*

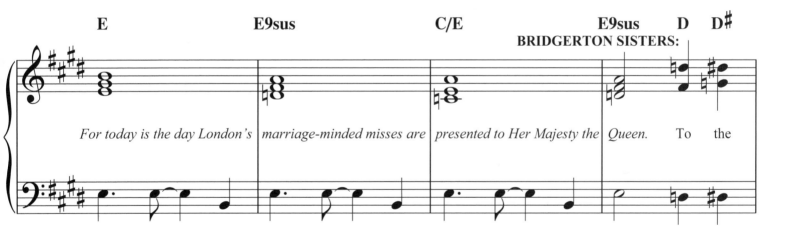

BRIDGERTON SISTERS:

For today is the day London's *marriage-minded misses are* *presented to Her Majesty the* *Queen.* To the

Queen!

HERALD:

Presenting ladies Prudence, *Philippa, and Penelope Featherington,* *all escorted by their mother,*

FEATHERINGTON SISTERS:

the Right Honorable   Lady Featherington.

Your Maj-es-

ty,   we're as per-fect as we   seem. Not the cake, but we're the

cream.Think I for-got how to   breathe!

LADY WHISTLEDOWN:

A glimmer of   displeasure, and a   young lady's value   plummets to   unthinkable

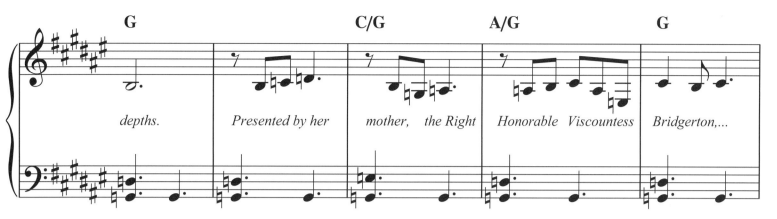

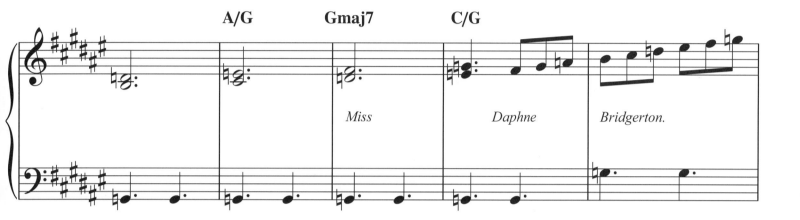

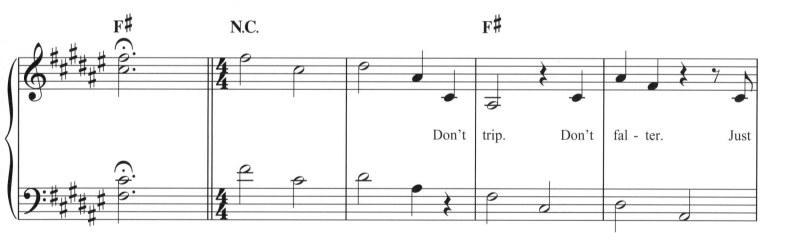

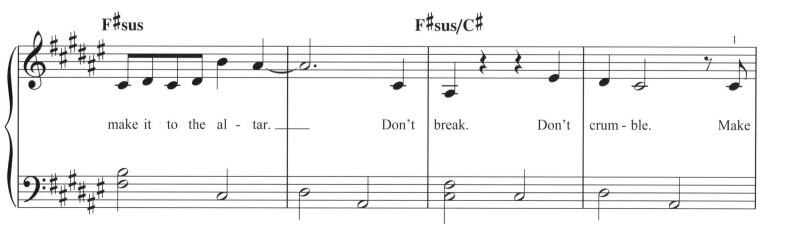

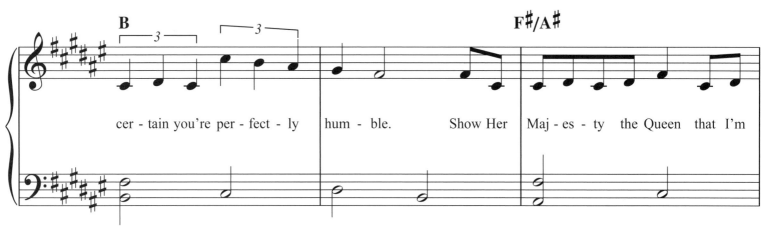

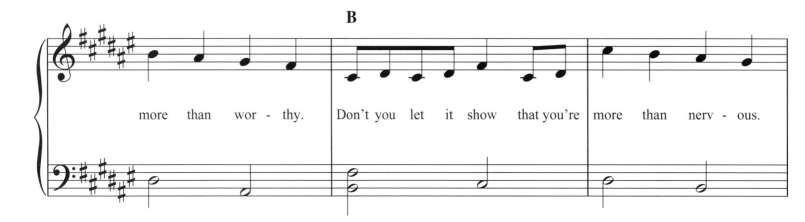

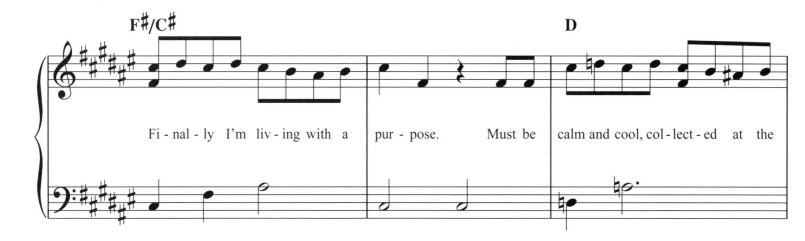

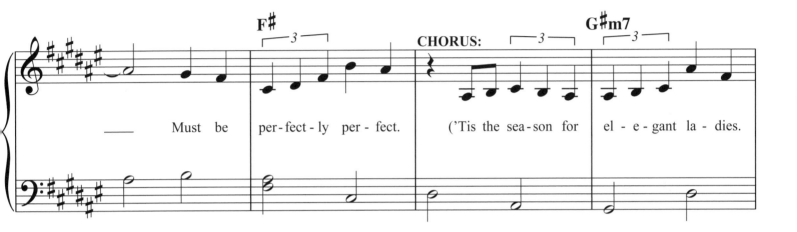

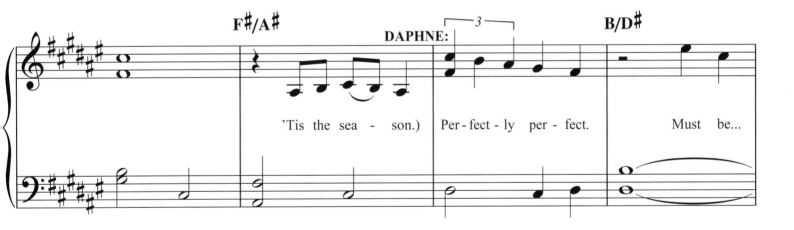

LADY WHISTLEDOWN

Words and Music by EMILY BEAR
and ABIGAIL BARLOW

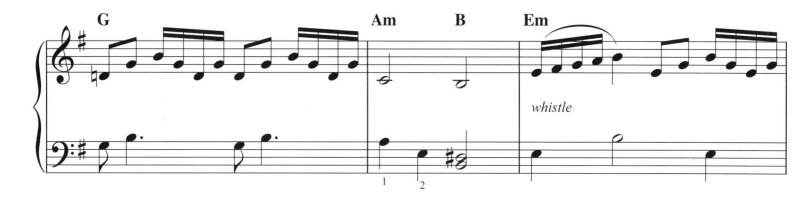

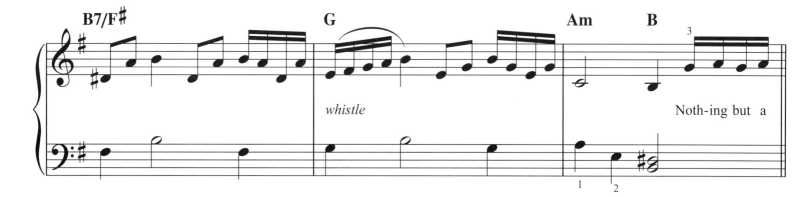

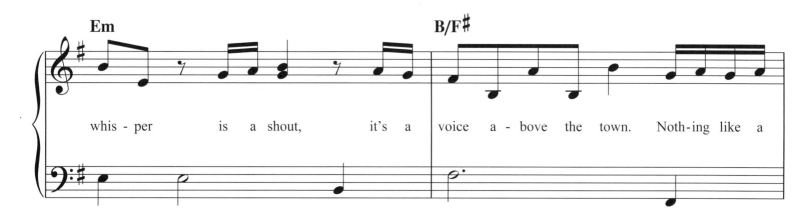

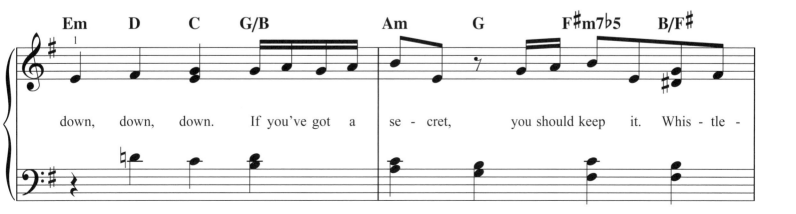

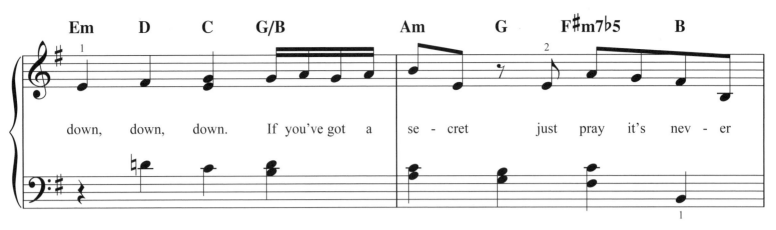

down, down, down. If you've got a se - cret just pray it's nev - er

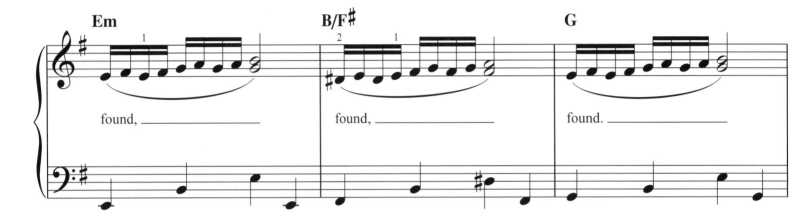

found, _____ found, _____ found. _____

Pray it's nev - er found, _____ found, _____

found. _____ With - out a doubt it's La - dy Whis - tle - down.

ALONE TOGETHER

Words and Music by EMILY BEAR
and ABIGAIL BARLOW

Moderately slow, in 1

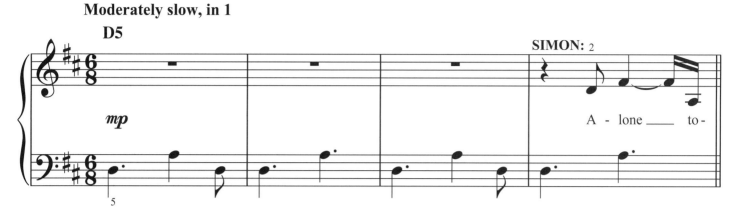

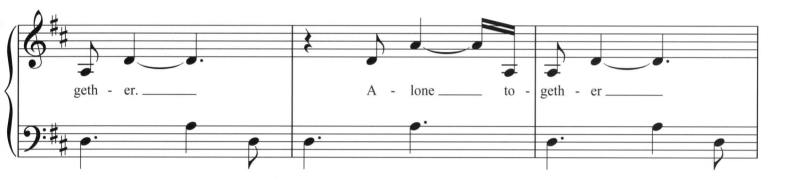

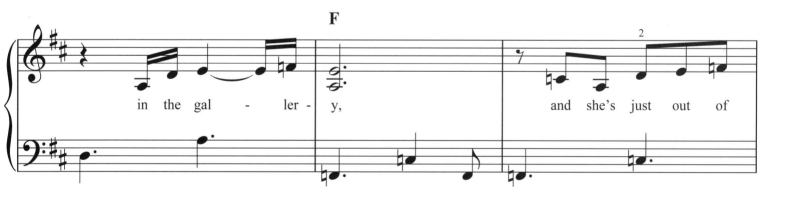

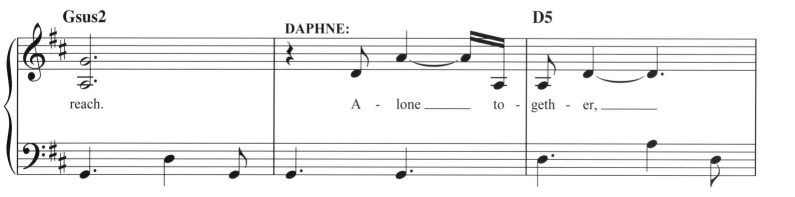

and just for a mo - ment, feels like I'll nev - er be ____ a - lone a -

F6/9

G

gain, I'll nev - er be ____ a - lone ____ a - gain. ____

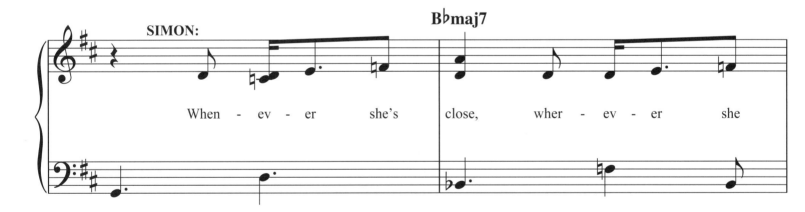

SIMON:

B♭maj7

When - ev - er she's close, wher - ev - er she

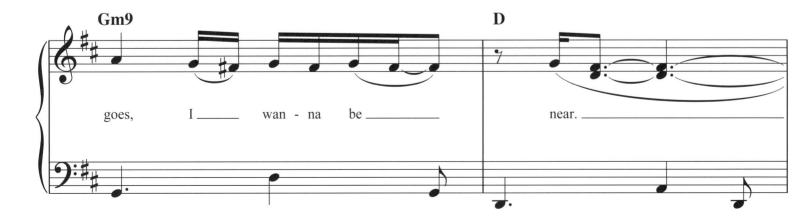

Gm9

D

goes, I ____ wan - na be ____ near. ____

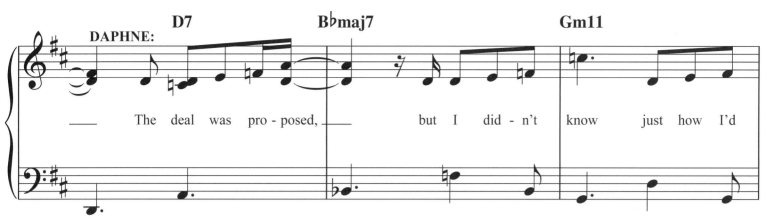

DAPHNE: The deal was pro - posed, but I did - n't know just how I'd

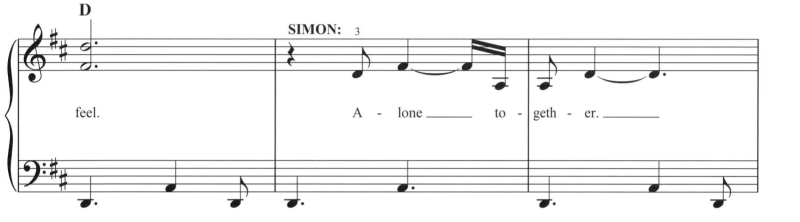

feel. **SIMON:** A - lone to - geth - er.

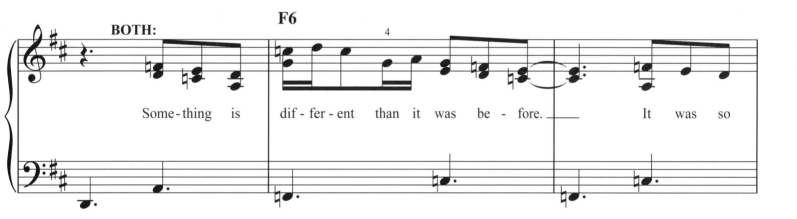

BOTH: Some - thing is dif - fer - ent than it was be - fore. It was so

in - no - cent; now that it's in - ti - mate, I want more.

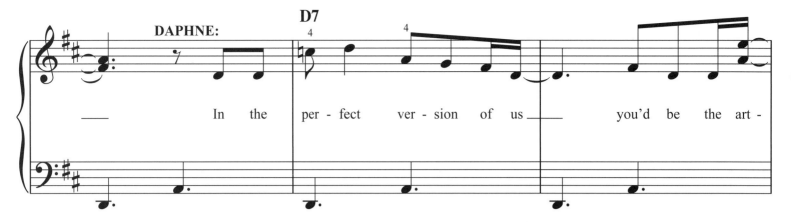

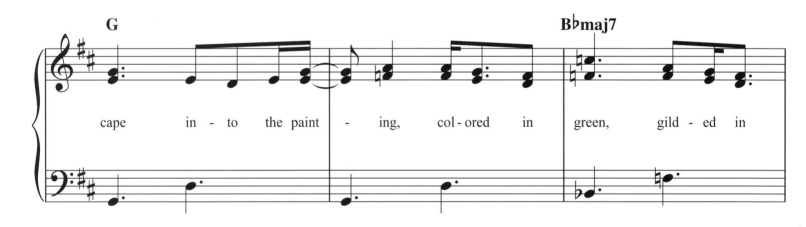

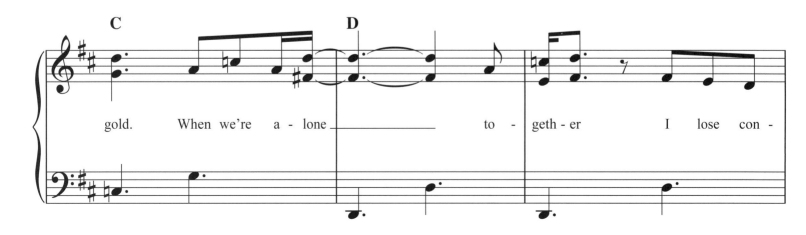

trol _____ when - ev - er our feel - ings un - fold the stor - ies we

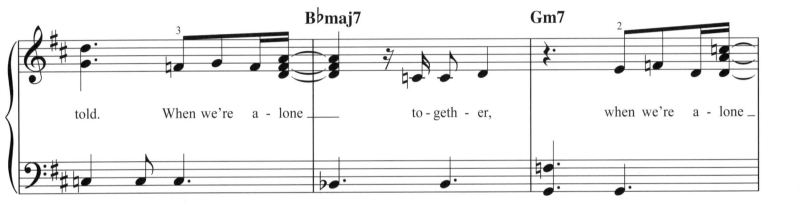

told. When we're a - lone _____ to - geth - er, when we're a - lone _

_____ to - geth - er I wish you were mine. _____

DAPHNE: *We should go.*   **SIMON:** *Right.*

IF I WERE A MAN

Words and Music by EMILY BEAR
and ABIGAIL BARLOW

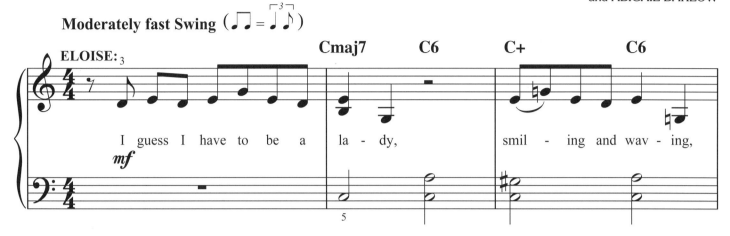

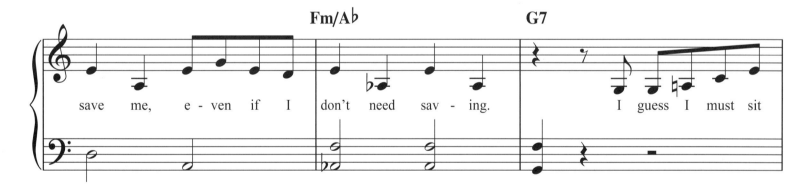

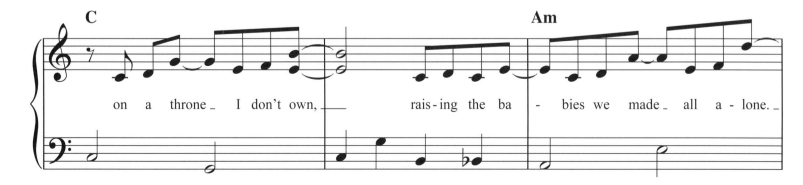

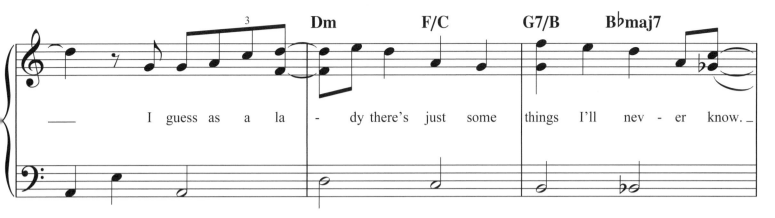

I guess as a la - dy there's just some things I'll nev - er know.

But if I were a man I'd go to Ja - pan,

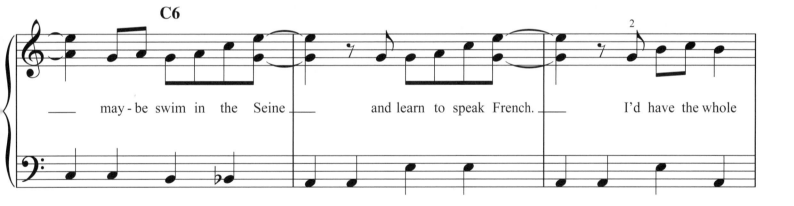

may - be swim in the Seine and learn to speak French. I'd have the whole

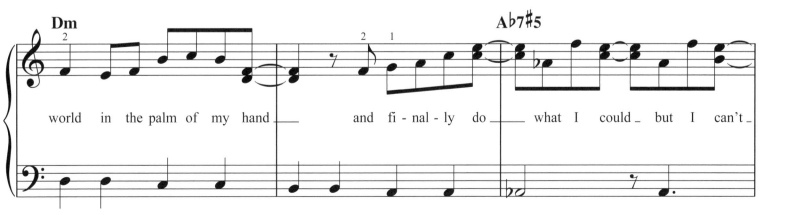

world in the palm of my hand and fi - nal - ly do what I could but I can't

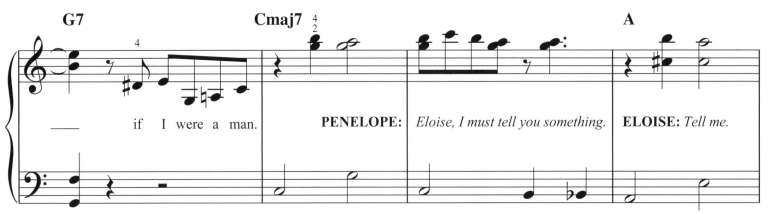

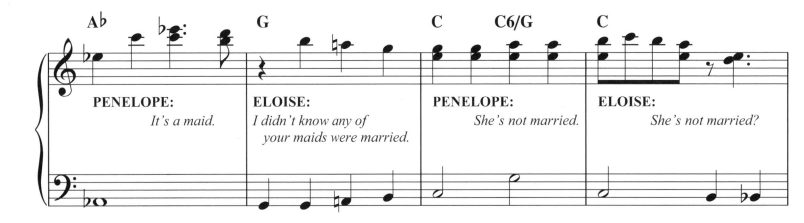

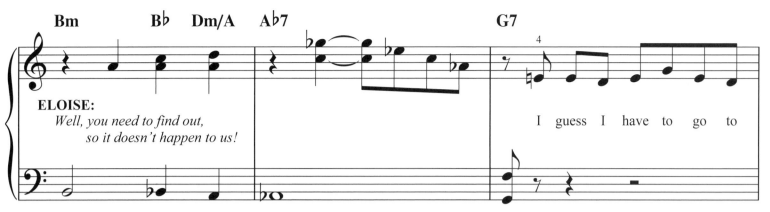

ELOISE:
*Well, you need to find out,
    so it doesn't happen to us!*

I guess I have to go to

ban - quets. Ban - quets make me anx - ious, act - ing rath - er shame - less.

I guess I need a gown down past my an - kles, do - ing up my

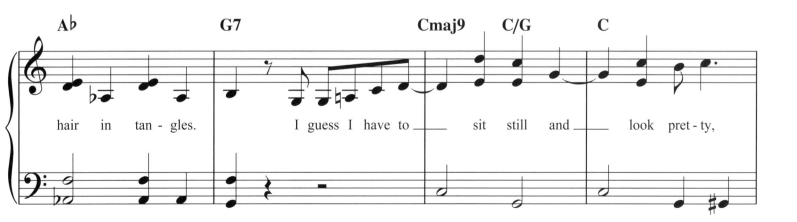

hair in tan - gles. I guess I have to ____ sit still and ____ look pret - ty,

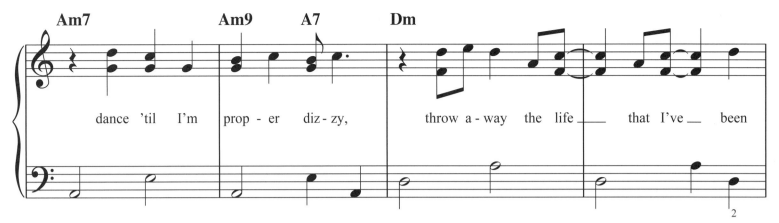

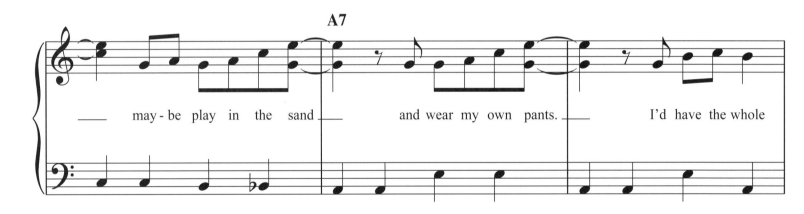

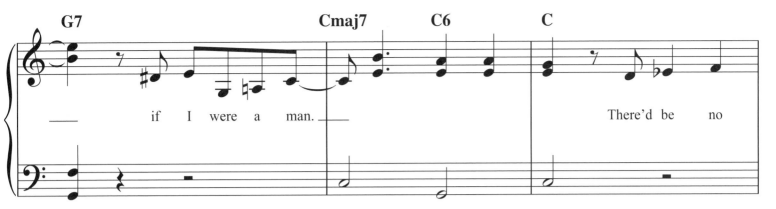

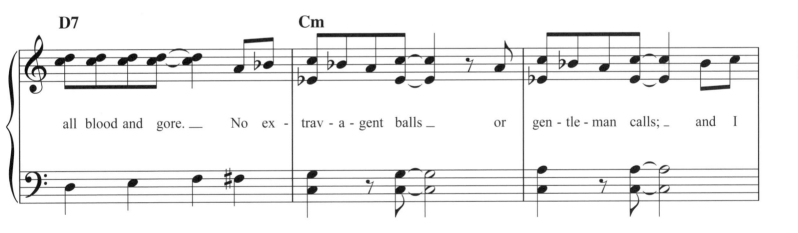

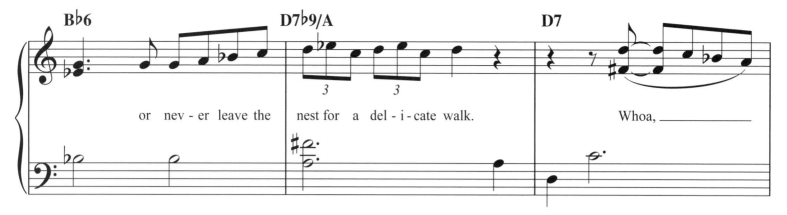

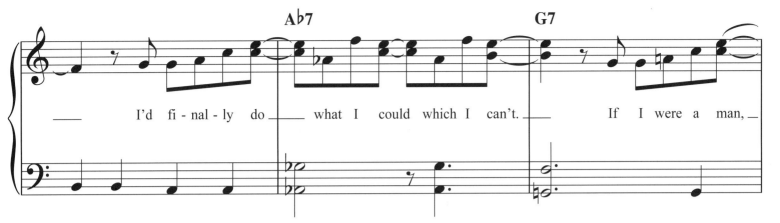

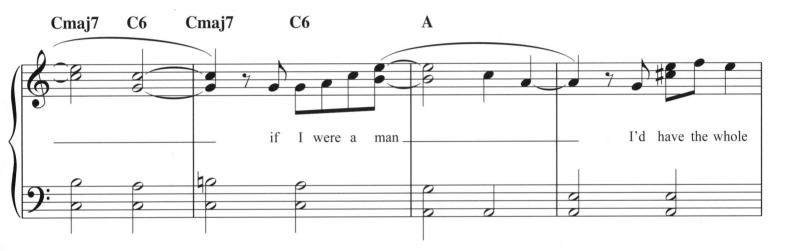

PENELOPE FEATHERINGTON

Words and Music by EMILY BEAR
and ABIGAIL BARLOW

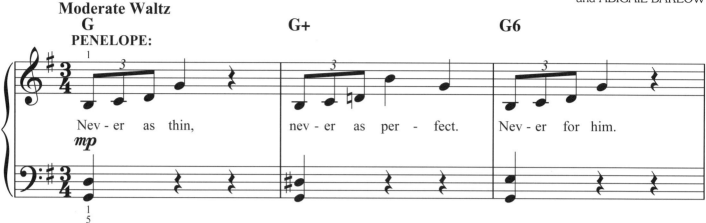

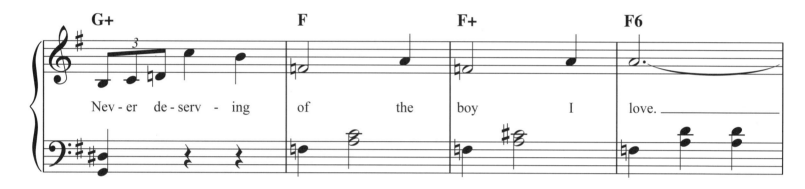

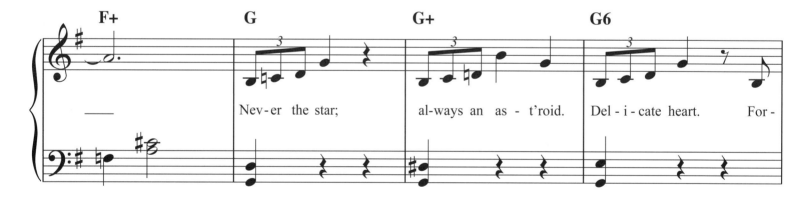

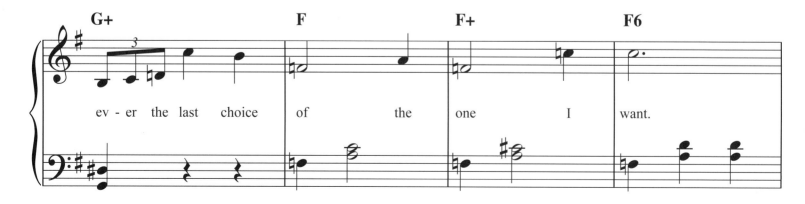

So I keep it all in. It's like I'm in -

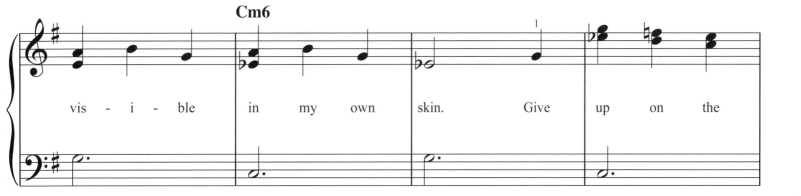

vis - i - ble in my own skin. Give up on the

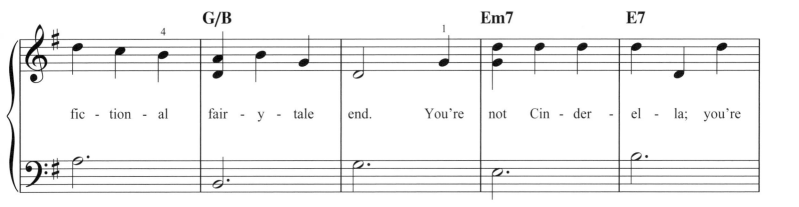

fic - tion - al fair - y - tale end. You're not Cin - der - el - la; you're

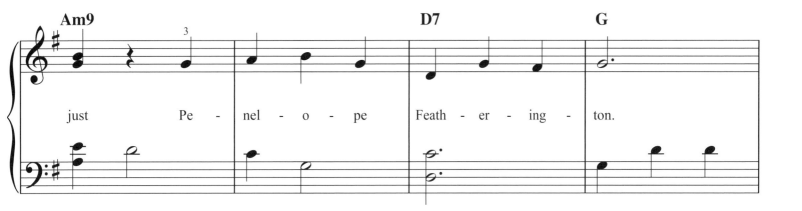

just Pe - nel - o - pe Feath - er - ing - ton.

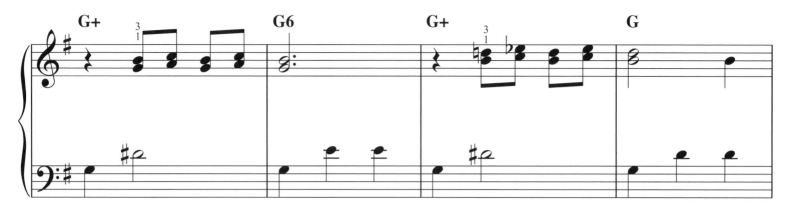

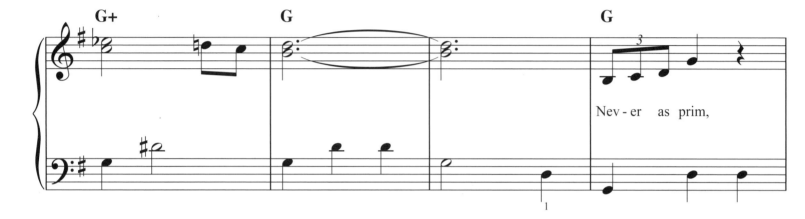

Nev - er as prim,

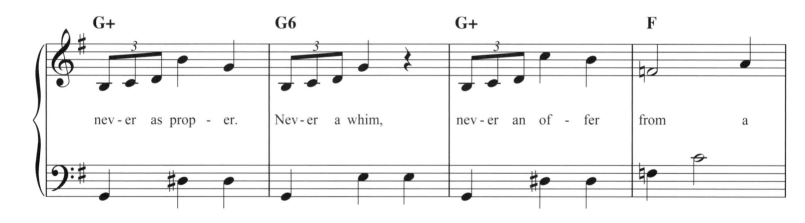

nev - er as prop - er. Nev - er a whim, nev - er an of - fer from a

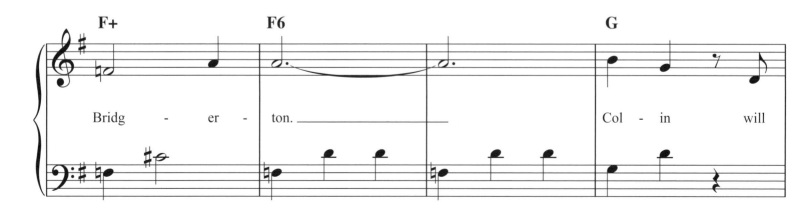

Bridg - er - ton. _____ Col - in will

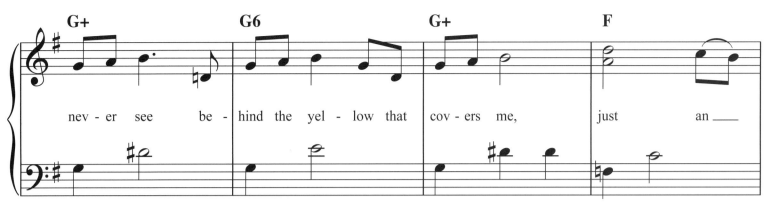

nev - er see be - hind the yel - low that cov - ers me, just an ___

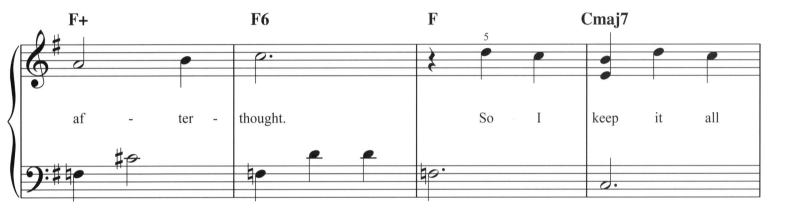

af - ter - thought. So I keep it all

in. It's like I'm in - vis - i - ble in my own

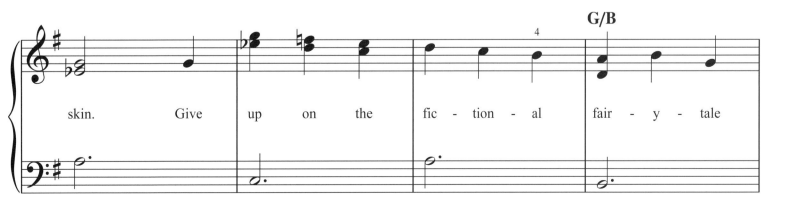

skin. Give up on the fic - tion - al fair - y - tale

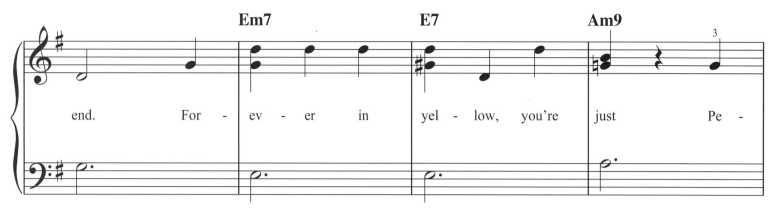

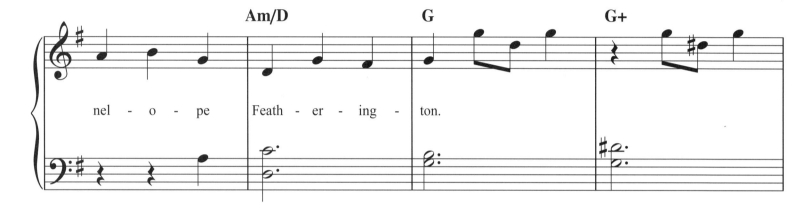

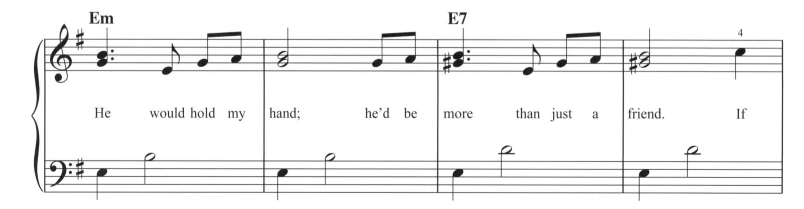

on - ly some - one else would just un - der - stand.

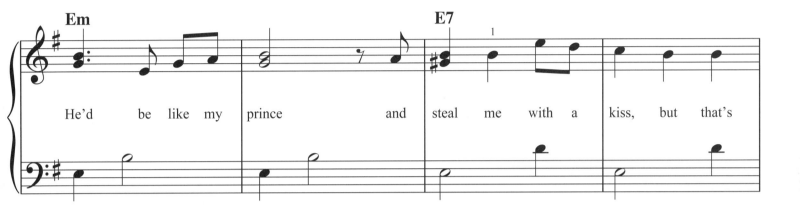

He'd be like my prince and steal me with a kiss, but that's

not real life: nev - er dressed in white. 'Cause I'm

Slightly slower

nev - er as thin, nev - er as per - fect. Nev - er for him. Nev - er de - serv - ing

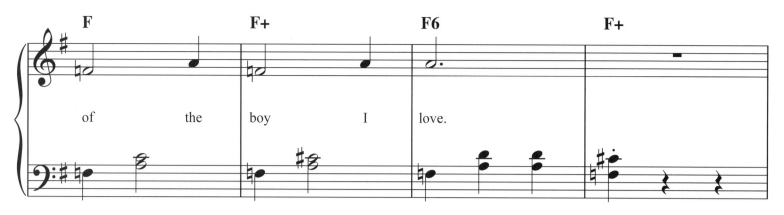

of the boy I love.

Slightly slower

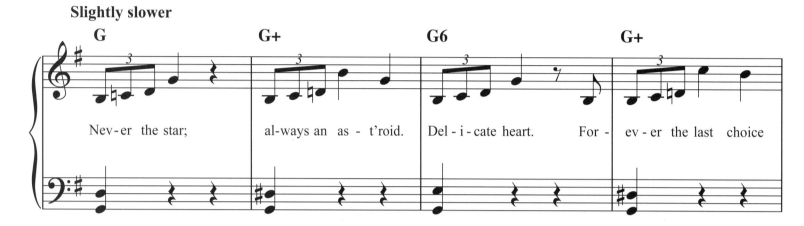

Nev-er the star; al-ways an as - t'roid. Del - i -cate heart. For - ev - er the last choice

of the one I want. So I

keep it all in. It's like I'm in - vis - i - ble

Adim/C   **Cm**

in   my   own   skin. ____   Give   up   on   the   fic - tion - al

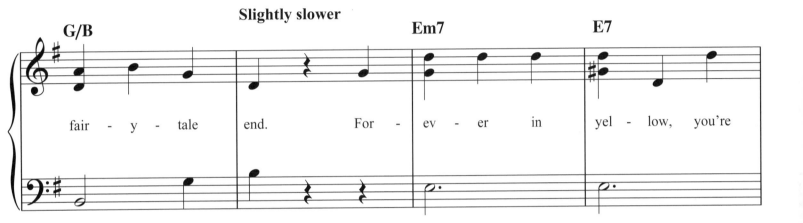

G/B   **Slightly slower**   **Em7**   **E7**

fair - y - tale   end.   For - ev - er   in   yel - low,   you're

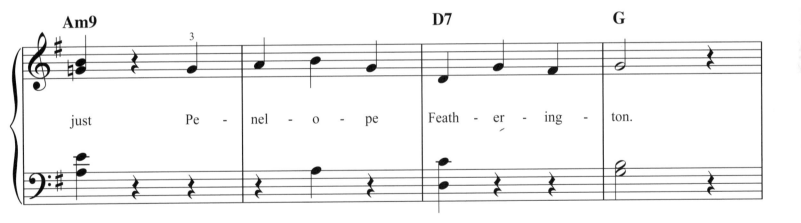

Am9   **D7**   **G**

just   Pe - nel - o - pe   Feath - er - ing - ton.

N.C.   **G**

FOOL FOR YOU

Words and Music by EMILY BEAR
and ABIGAIL BARLOW

With a groove

No, don't you try to hold me close. That door is closed now.

Go, go find your-self a girl who smells just like a rose. I'm on my own now.

I don't need you, you don't need me, I can fight my own bat - tles.

And I ___ won't be a fool for you. ___ I ___ won't be a fool no

41

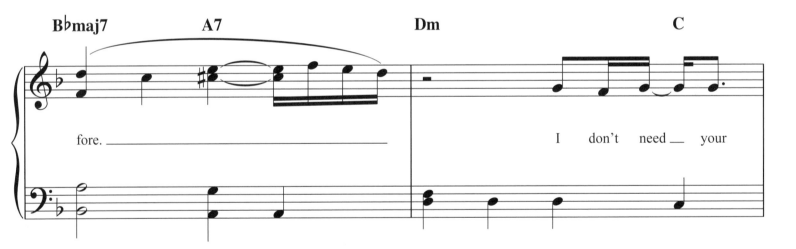

ENTERTAIN ME

Words and Music by EMILY BEAR
and ABIGAIL BARLOW

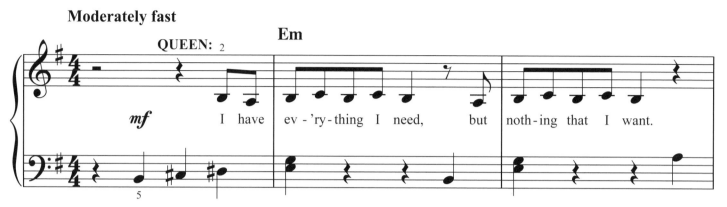

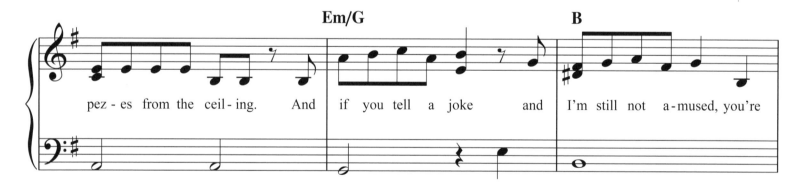

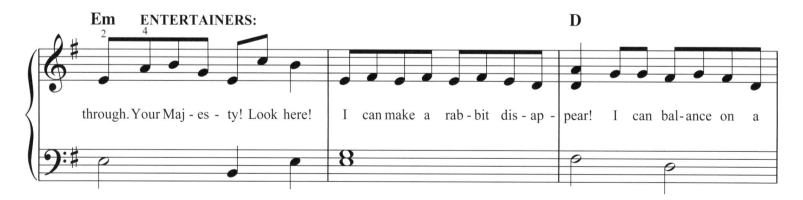

COURTIER:

En - ter - tain!   En - ter - tain! Where's my snuff? Where's my flask?   Your

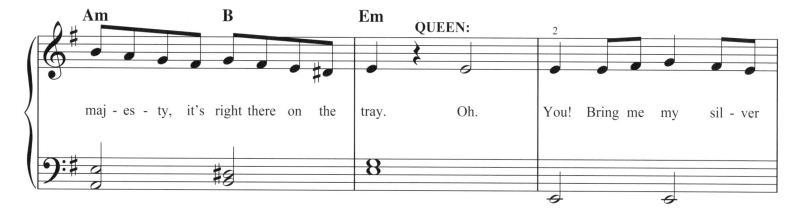

QUEEN:

maj - es - ty, it's right there on the tray.   Oh.   You! Bring me my sil - ver

spoon,   and while you're at it, pre - pare a goose, and tell the

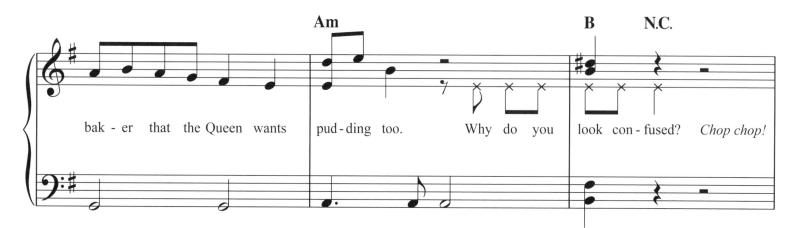

bak - er that the Queen wants pud - ding too.   Why do you look con - fused? *Chop chop!*

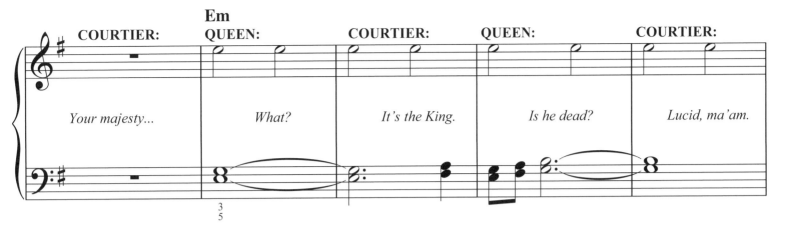

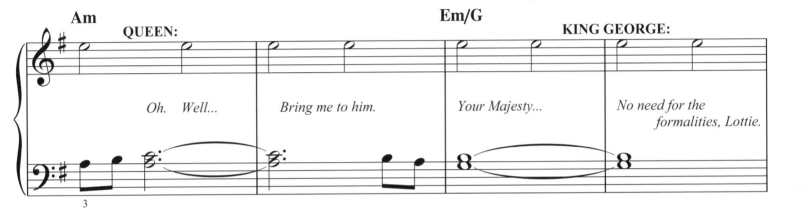

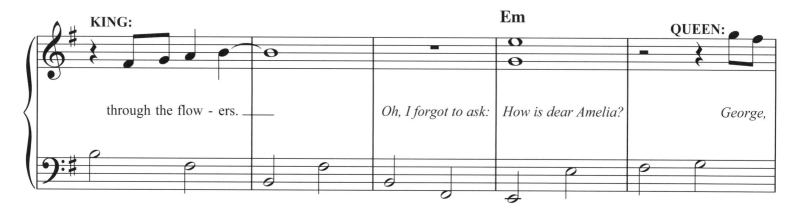

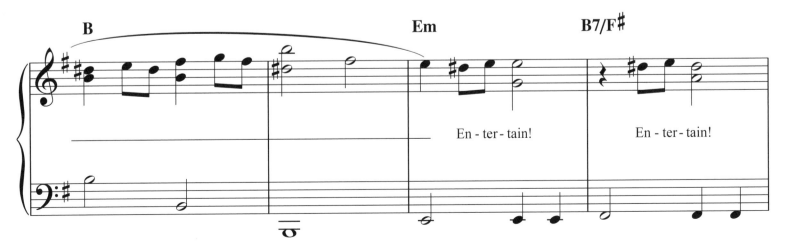

48

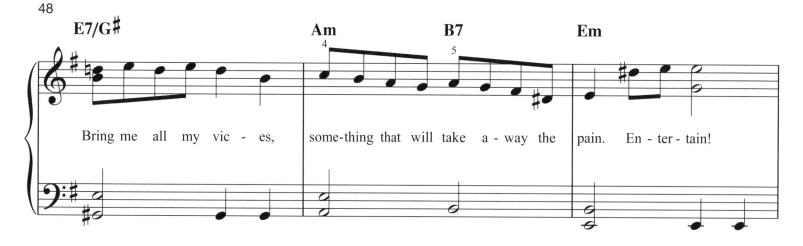

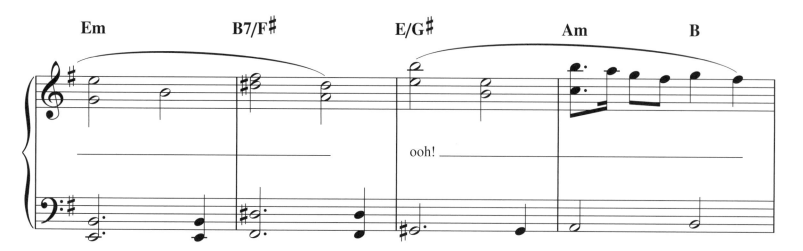

CROWD:
She's not liv - ing, just sur - viv - ing. No more liv - ing. Your san - i - ty is cir - cl - ing the

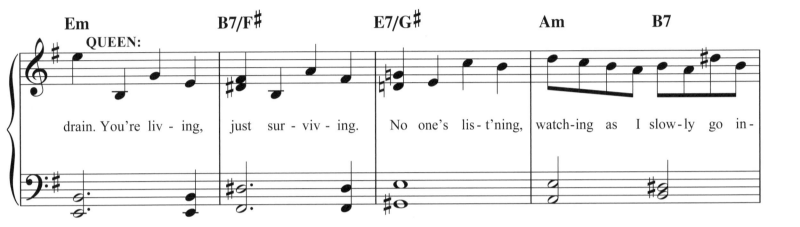

QUEEN:
drain. You're liv - ing, just sur - viv - ing. No one's lis - t'ning, watch - ing as I slow - ly go in -

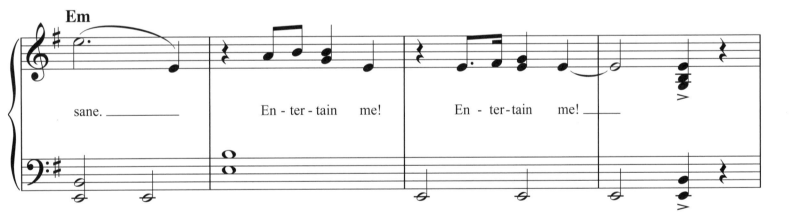

sane. _____ En - ter - tain me! En - ter - tain me! _____

COURTIER: QUEEN: COURTIER: QUEEN:
Your Majesty... What? ***p*** *It's the latest Whistledown.* *Hmm... That will do!*

FRIEND TURNED FOE

Words and Music by EMILY BEAR
and ABIGAIL BARLOW

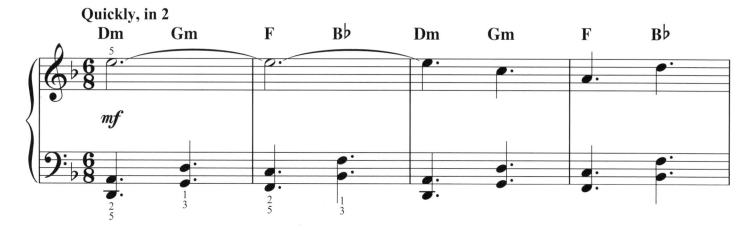

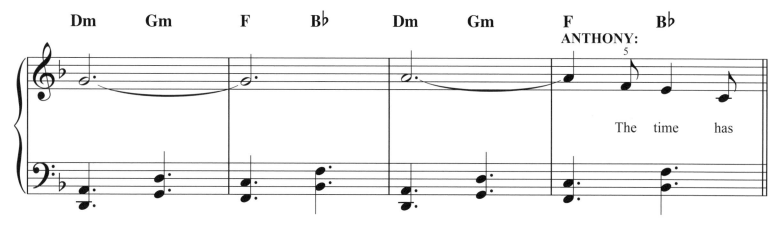

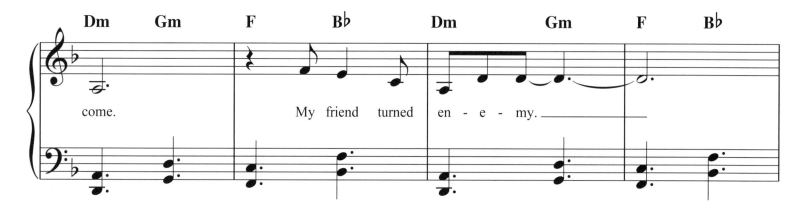

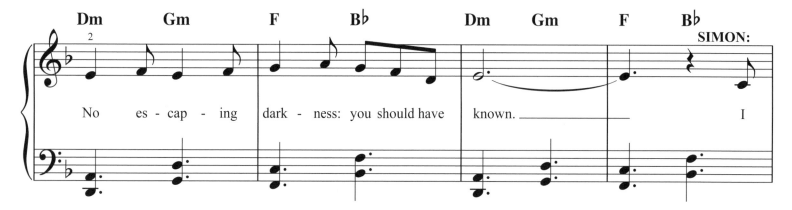

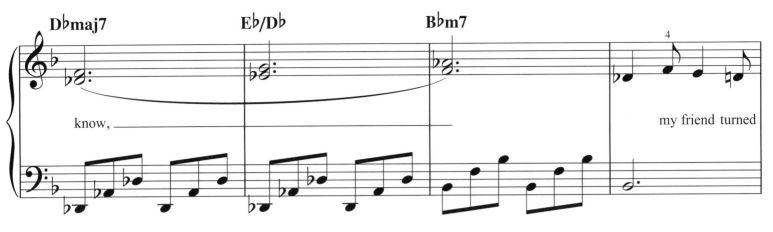

know, _____ my friend turned

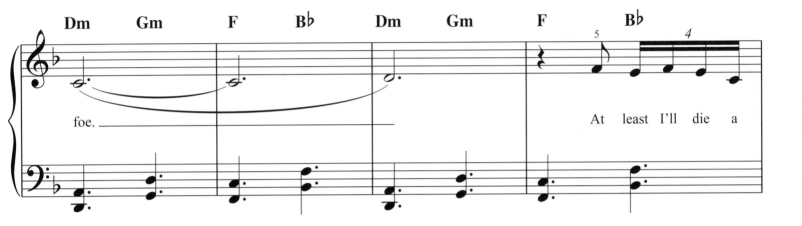

foe. _____ At least I'll die a

man. At least I'll die with hon - or now. _____ It's

guar - an - teed there'll nev - er be an heir of my

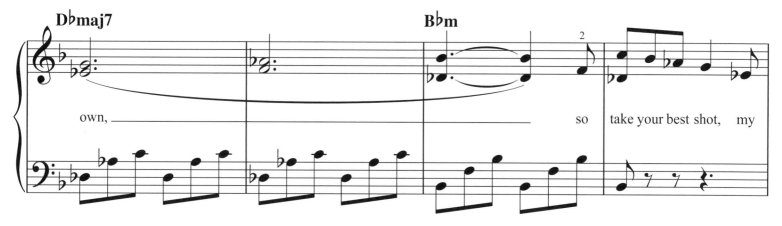

own, _____ so take your best shot, my

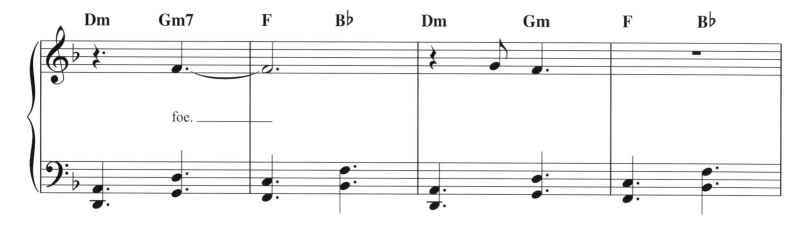

foe. _____

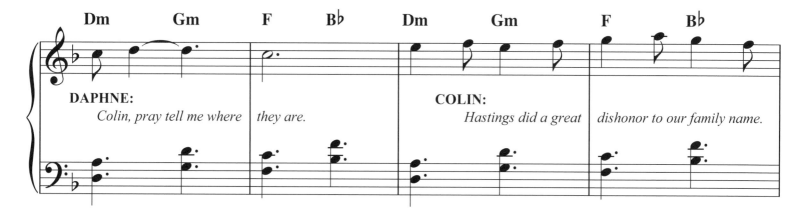

DAPHNE:
Colin, pray tell me where they are.

COLIN:
Hastings did a great dishonor to our family name.

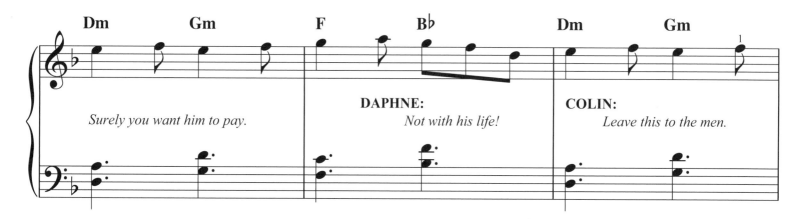

Surely you want him to pay.

DAPHNE:
Not with his life!

COLIN:
Leave this to the men.

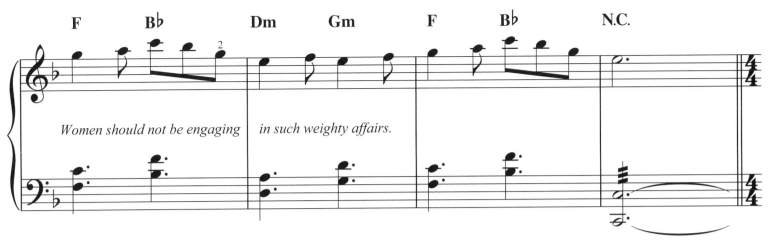

Women should not be engaging | *in such weighty affairs.*

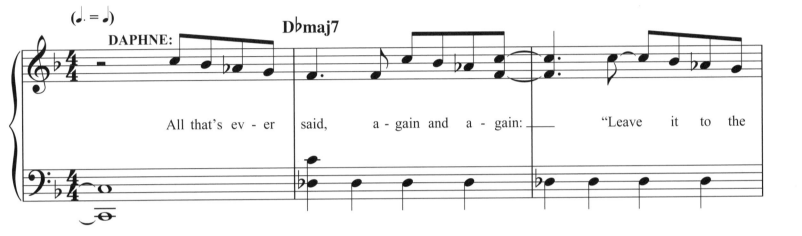

DAPHNE: All that's ev - er said, a - gain and a - gain: ____ "Leave it to the

men!" To de - scend ____ in - to mad - ness. But what if that mad - ness is

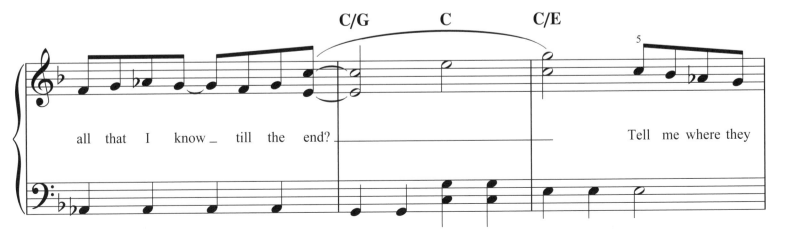

all that I know ____ till the end? ____ Tell me where they

went, Col - in. _____ Tell ___ me where they went, broth - er.

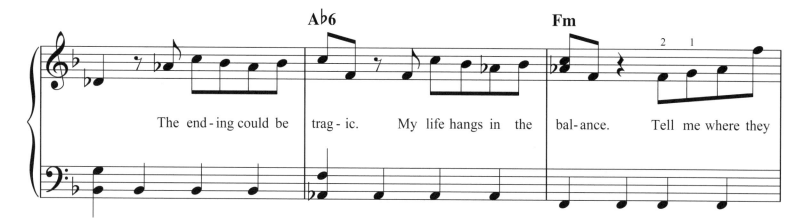

The end - ing could be trag - ic. My life hangs in the bal - ance. Tell me where they

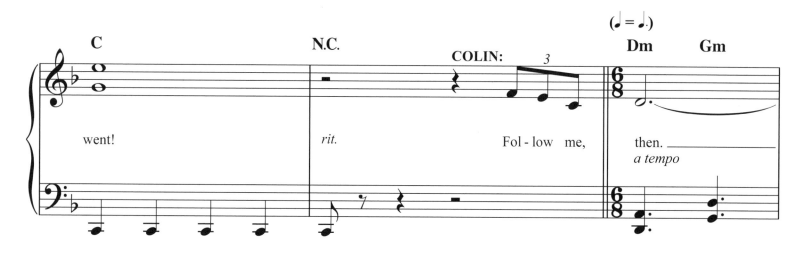

went! *rit.* **COLIN:** Fol - low me, then. _____ *a tempo*

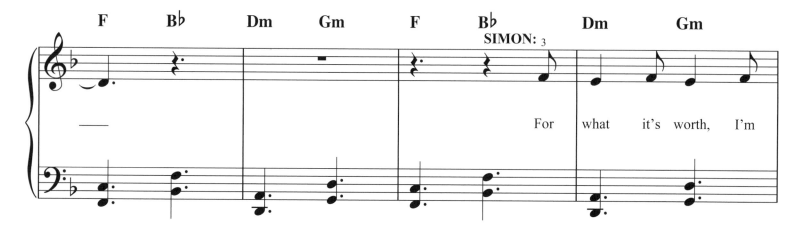

SIMON: For what it's worth, I'm

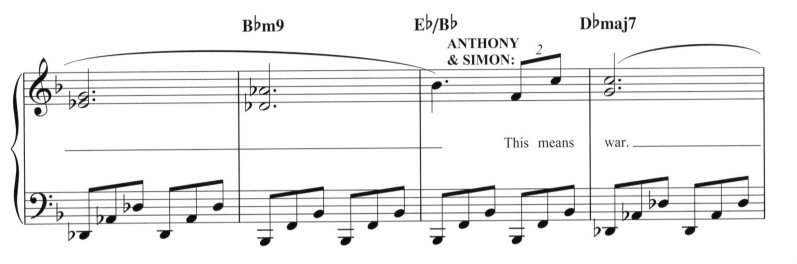

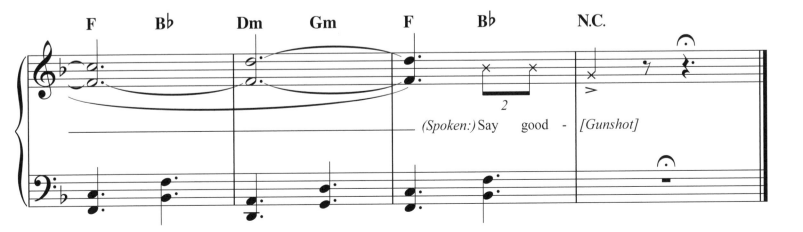

BURN FOR YOU

Words and Music by EMILY BEAR
and ABIGAIL BARLOW

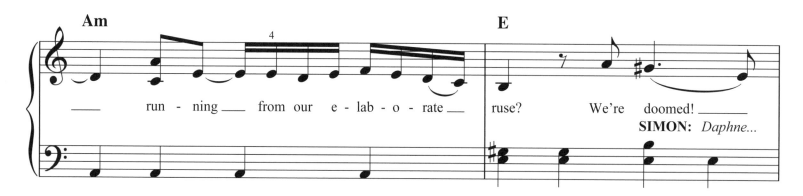

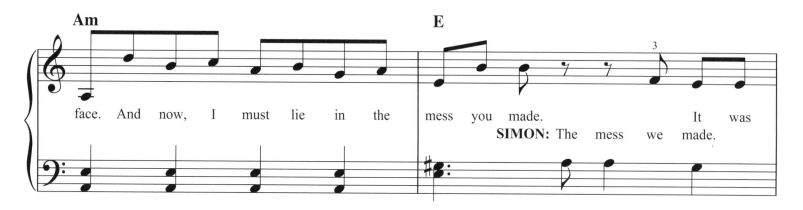

your mis - take; you kissed me in the maze. I was pre-pared to take my

life. I stole your fate. I stole your fate. I stole your fate. No, I stole ___ your

fate! (Spoken:) I don't understand. And now, you're forced to love a man ___ you hate. Simon... I

know you don't feel the same, but I burn ___

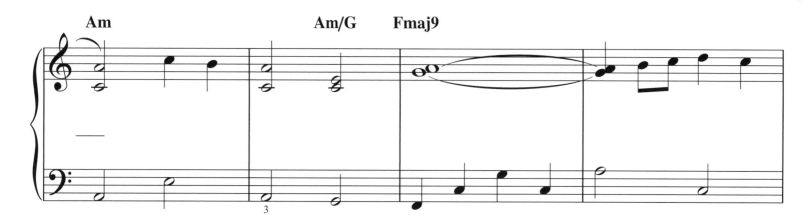

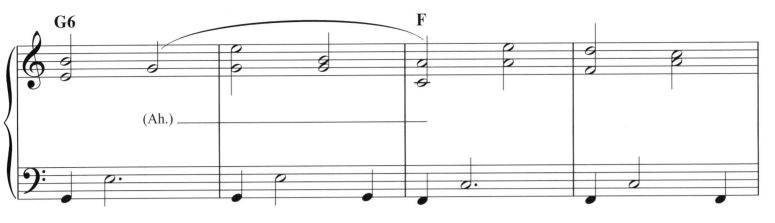

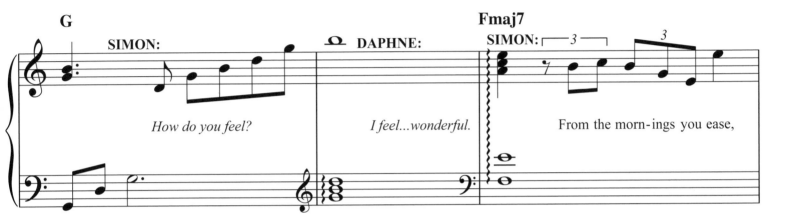

Dm6 ... **Am** ... **G6**

night, it is you I can-not sac-ri-fice. Look me in my eyes! I

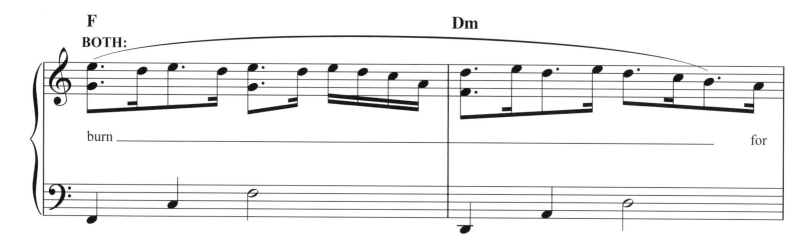

F **Dm**

BOTH:

burn _____ for

Am **E** **F**

DAPHNE: BOTH:

you, I burn for you. I ___ burn, I burn _____

Dm **Am** **E**

_____ for you. I burn, I burn. ___

EVERY INCH

Words and Music by EMILY BEAR
and ABIGAIL BARLOW

light, she is mu - sic. She is mine. I could

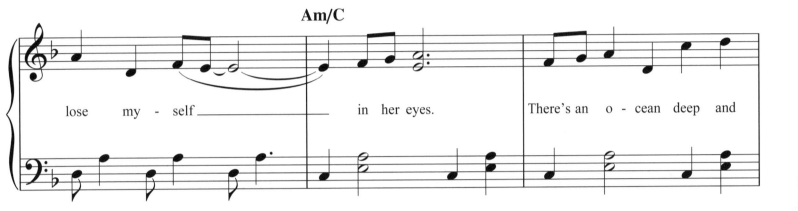

lose my - self in her eyes. There's an o - cean deep and

wide, and I'm be - ing pulled by the tide.

She's a mel - o - dy, she's a muse, she's a rem - e - dy

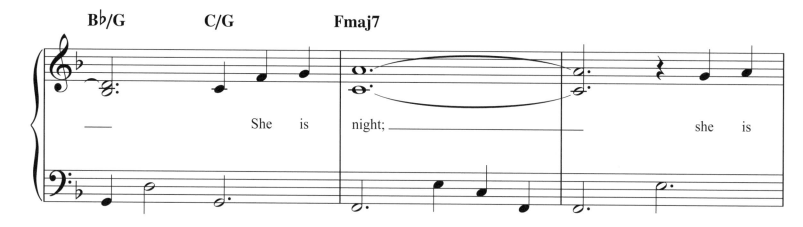

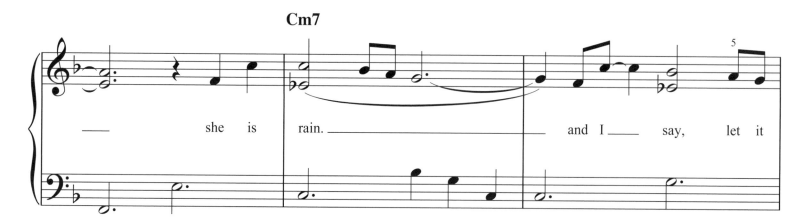

B♭maj7   **A♭6/9**

pour.   I   have   been   wait   -   ing   for ____

A♭   **Fmaj7/E**

some - one   like   her,

Dm7

some-thing   like   this. _____   I'm   in

F/C   **B♭(add2)**

love   with   you, ___   ev - er - y   inch   of   you.

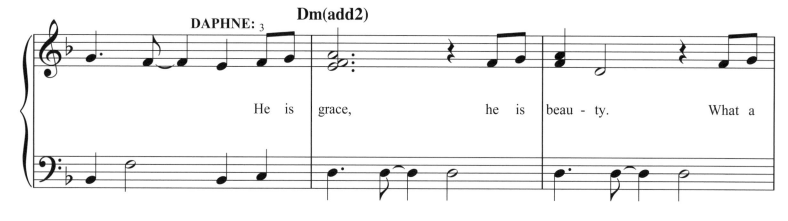

DAPHNE: Dm(add2)

He is grace, he is beau-ty. What a

Dm9/C   B♭maj7

face! I could lose my-self ___ in his em-brace. He's an

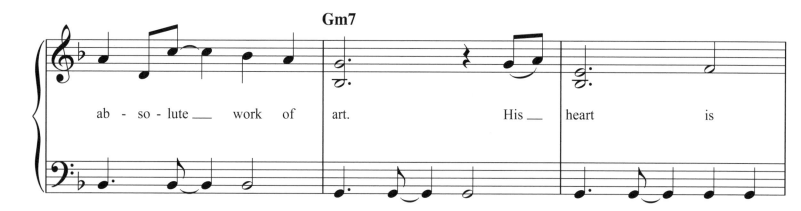

Gm7

ab-so-lute ___ work of art. His ___ heart is

Dm(add2)

beat-ing just ___ for me. I can hard-ly breathe. Fell

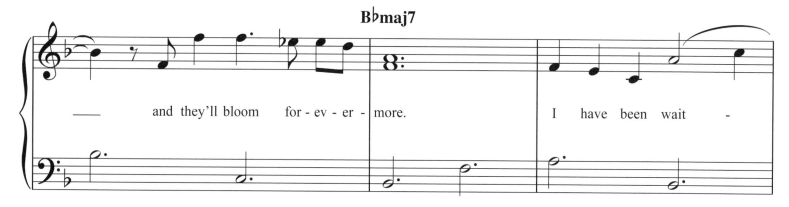

and they'll bloom for-ev-er-more. I have been wait -

- ing for ___ some-one like him,

some-thing like this. ___ I'm

in love with him, ev-er-y inch of him. ___

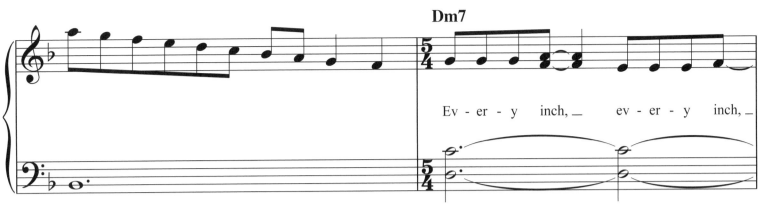

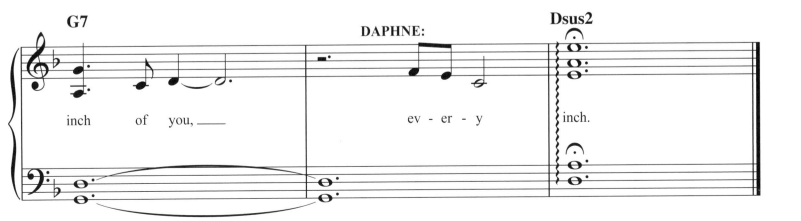

BALANCING THE SCALES

Words and Music by EMILY BEAR
and ABIGAIL BARLOW

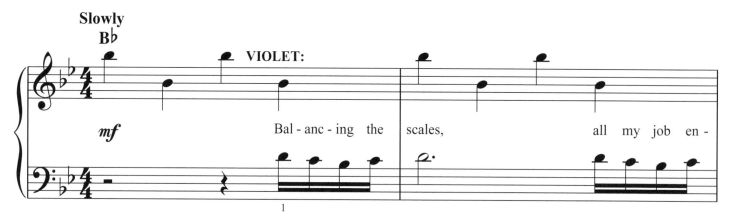

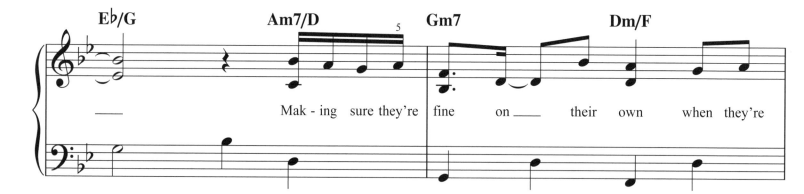

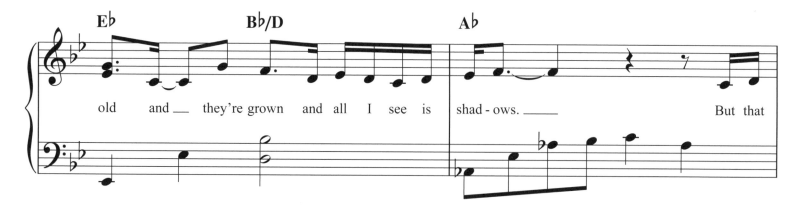

doesn't make it eas-i-er to let them go. Ooh. _____

_____ I walk past the doors and the cor-ri-dors where they

grew, and all I feel is emp-ti-ness _____ from this

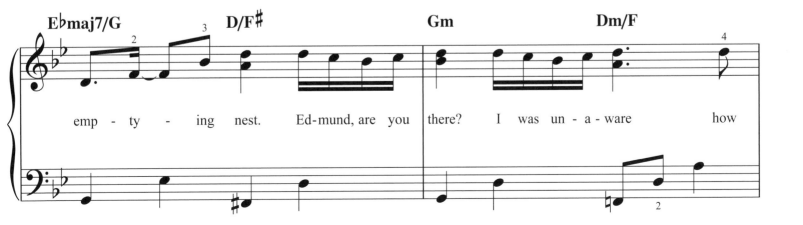

emp-ty-ing nest. Ed-mund, are you there? I was un-a-ware how

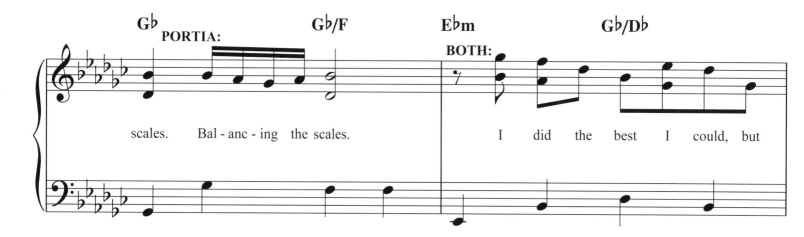

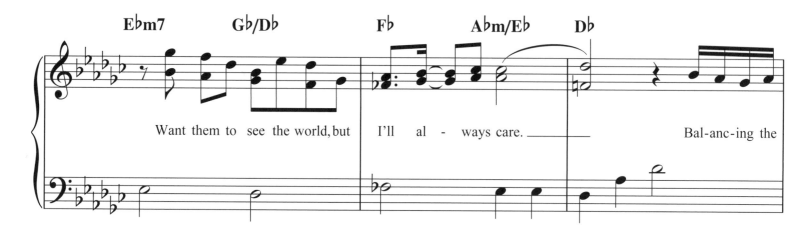

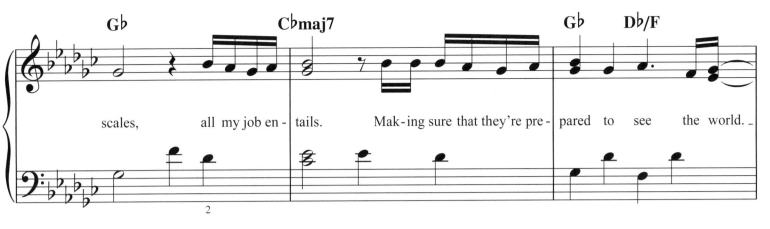

scales, all my job en - tails. Mak-ing sure that they're pre - pared to see the world. _

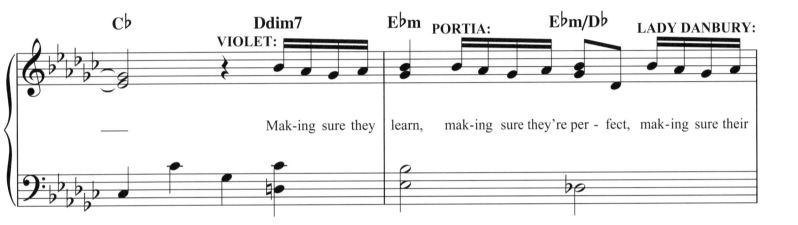

VIOLET:
_____ Mak-ing sure they learn, mak-ing sure they're per - fect, mak-ing sure their

PORTIA:

LADY DANBURY:

worth is al - ways some-thing that they know. But it

ALL 3:

does-n't make it eas - i - er to let them go.

8vb

OCEAN AWAY

Words and Music by EMILY BEAR
and ABIGAIL BARLOW

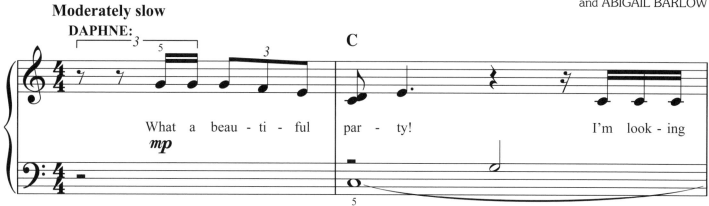

What a beau-ti-ful par-ty! I'm look-ing

up at the ceil-ing a lot. The chan-de-lier is so spark-ly. You nev-er said

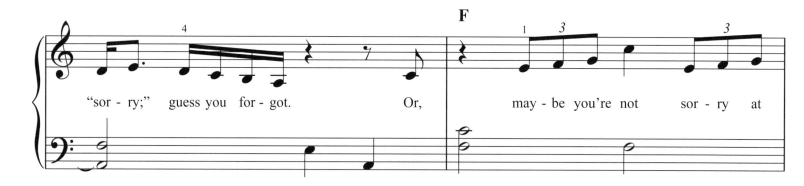

"sor-ry;" guess you for-got. Or, may-be you're not sor-ry at

all. But, a beau-ti-ful eve-ning. I want to know, just what the hell you are think-

ing. Oh so sto - ic, e - mo-tion-less, o - ver us all so quick- ly. What am I

miss-ing? I ____ can't e -ven drink cham - pagne, no, ____ with-out see -ing your ____

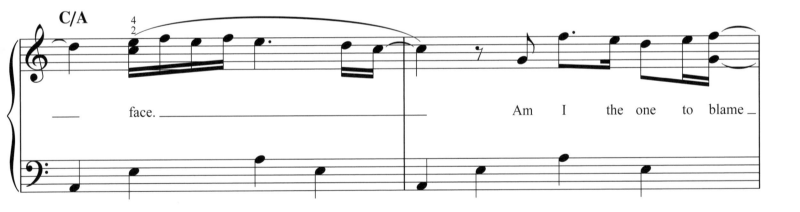

____ face. ____ Am I the one to blame ____

____ when we're danc - ing in the same room ____ and you're an o - cean a -

way?

SIMON: What a ter - ri - ble *soi - rée,* with

ter - ri - ble peo - ple pre-tend - ing they're hap - py in this mas - quer - ade. _ We go _

_ through the mo - tions when all _ that we wish _ is es - cape _ from the choic - es we

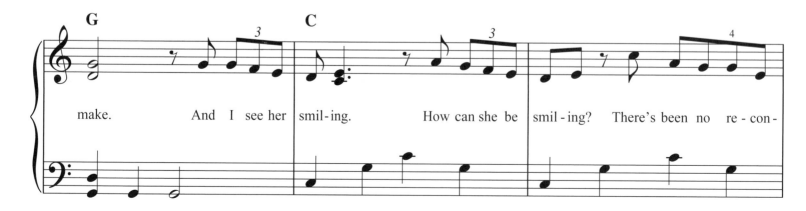

make. And I see her smil - ing. How can she be smil - ing? There's been no re - con-

cil - ing.   And when she's ___ at my fo - cus, she won't e - ven no - tice my

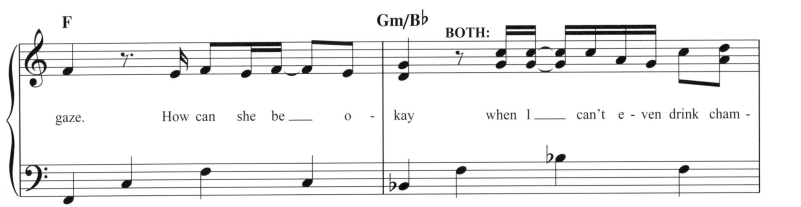

gaze.   How can she be __ o - kay   when I __ can't e - ven drink cham -

pagne,   no, __ with-out see - ing __ your __ face? _____

__ Am I __ the one __ to blame ____ when we're danc -

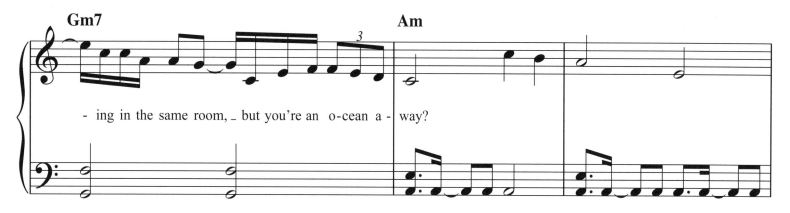

- ing in the same room, _ but you're an o-cean a - way?

For - get the ache _ of yes - ter - day, _ and why _

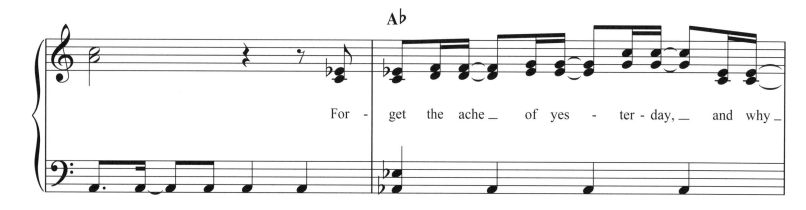

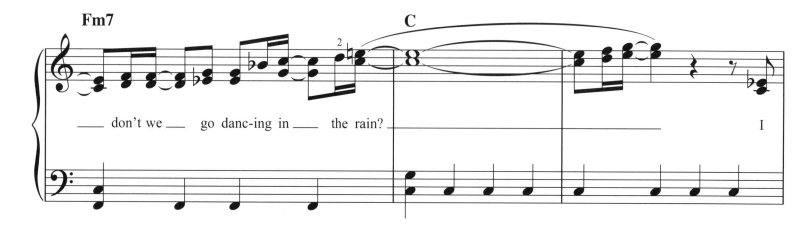

_ don't we _ go danc-ing in _ the rain? _ I

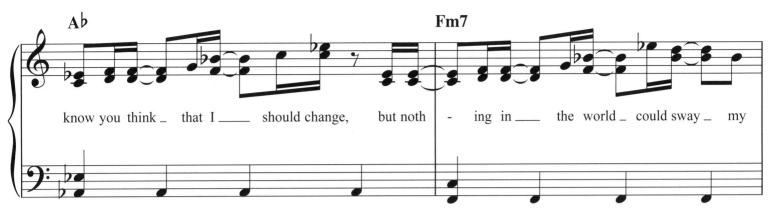

know you think _ that I _____ should change, but noth - ing in _____ the world _ could sway _ my

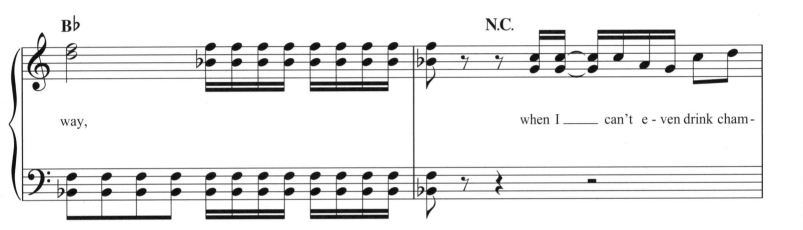

way, when I _____ can't e - ven drink cham-

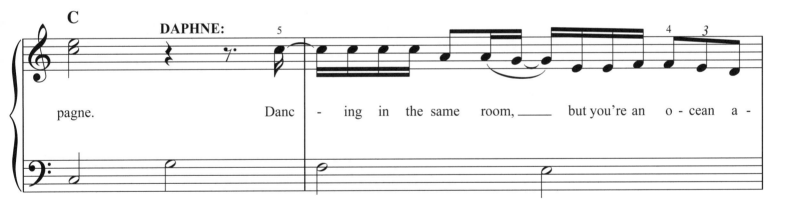

DAPHNE:

pagne. Danc - ing in the same room, _____ but you're an o - cean a -

BOTH:

way. You're an o-cean a - way. _____ I _____

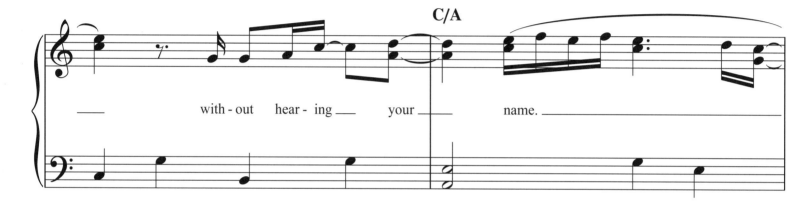